creative director **Susie Garland Rice**
art direction & story adaptation **Shannon Osborne Thompson**

Dalmatian Press owns all art and editorial material.
ISBN: 1-57759-272-7
© 1999 Dalmatian Press. All rights reserved.
Printed and bound in the U.S.A. The DALMATIAN PRESS name,
logo and spotted spine are trademarks of Dalmatian Press, Franklin, Tennessee 37067.
Written permission must be secured from the publisher to use or reproduce any part of this book.

Noah's Ark

Illustrated by
Sherry Neidigh

Dalmatian
Press

God told Noah to build an ark
with one window and one door.

Then he told Noah to put two of every kind of animal on the ark.

God sent the animals to Noah
two by two.

There were two elephants

and two mice,

two toucans

and two lions,

two giraffes

and two pandas,

two tigers

and two kangaroos,

two hippopotamuses

and two penguins,

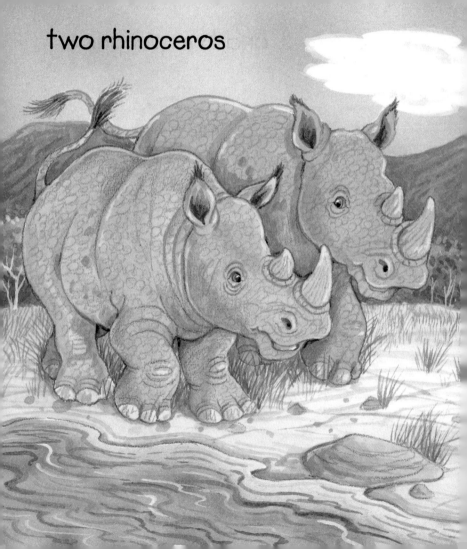

two rhinoceros

and two zebras,

and two of every other animal.
Two by two the animals went
aboard the ark.

Then it started to rain. It rained and rained until all the earth was covered with water.

After forty days the rain stopped and Noah sent out a dove.

When the dove returned
with an olive branch, Noah
knew there was dry land.

Finally, Noah opened the door to let all the animals off the ark.

And there in the sky was a
rainbow, a sign of God's promise
that a flood would never again
destroy the whole earth.

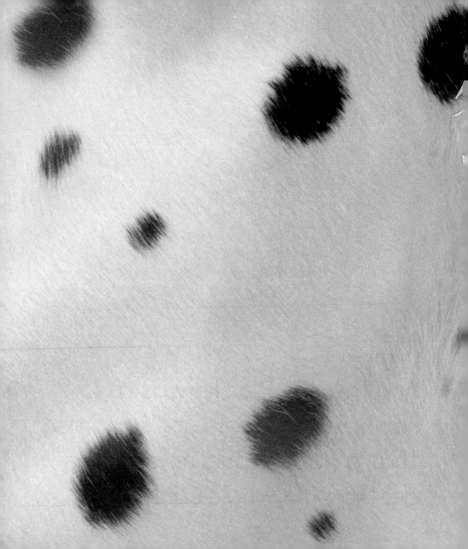